CHARACTER
WITNESSES

MIKE GILLESPIE

VICTOR BOOKS

A DIVISION OF SCRIPTURE PRESS PUBLICATIONS INC.
USA CANADA ENGLAND

Other Young Teen Feedback Electives

CROSS TRAINING
FAMILY SURVIVAL GUIDE
FOR REAL PEOPLE ONLY
FRIENDS – WHO NEEDS THEM?
IT CAME FROM THE MEDIA
NOBODY LIKE ME
THE SCHOOL ZONE
WHAT'S YOUR PROBLEM?
WHEN EVERYONE'S LOOKING AT YOU

Leader's books available for group study.

Scripture quotations are from the *Holy Bible, New International Version*, © 1973, 1978, 1984, International Bible Society. Used by permission of Zondervan Bible Publishers.

Library of Congress Catalog Card Number: 90-72086
ISBN: 0-89693-838-7

1 2 3 4 5 6 7 8 9 10 Printing/Year 95 94 93 92 91

© 1991, SP Publications, Inc. All rights reserved. Printed in the United States of America.

CONTENTS

INTRODUCTION   5

PART 1: BUILDING THE FOUNDATION

   CHAPTER 1   "BUT EVERYONE CHEATS"   7

   CHAPTER 2   ON-THE-JOB TRAINING   15

   CHAPTER 3   A TRUE TEST OF CHARACTER   22

   CHAPTER 4   RISKING YOUR LIFE OVER RESPECT   30

PART 2: THE POWER OF MOTIVATION

   CHAPTER 5   STANDING ALONE   38

   CHAPTER 6   JUST WAIT A LITTLE WHILE LONGER   46

   CHAPTER 7   IT'S GOING TO TAKE MORE THAN LEGO BLOCKS   55

   CHAPTER 8   THOSE GRUMBLING HEBREWS   63

PART 3: BUILDING SPIRITUAL MUSCLES

   CHAPTER 9   A VERY SPECIAL WOMAN   69

   CHAPTER 10   WALKING ON HOLY GROUND   76

   CHAPTER 11   LOPSIDED ODDS   81

   CHAPTER 12   THE GREATEST OF THESE   90

INTRODUCTION

Wanted: Teenagers with Christian character. Great character! Applications available.

Think about the people you admire. Why do you admire them?
- Good looks?
- Clothes?
- Status?
- Money?
- Achievements?
- Sex Appeal?
- Intelligence?
- Talent?
- Etc.

Would you want people to use that list to evaluate you? What if you didn't have any of that stuff?

Good news. There's another list. A special one made of Christian qualities. It's called character.

This book is about that. It's your application form. When you finish, you will have discovered 12 essential character traits for a Christian teenager.

You may have some or all of them already. It will be fun deciding which ones you possess and which ones you've never even seen close to your life.

Want to be the best you can be? Wear these 12 traits. You will become a great witness for your faith. Best of all you won't even know it. But God will.

PART 1: BUILDING THE FOUNDATION

"BUT EVERYONE CHEATS"
CHAPTER ONE

The story is told of a well-dressed bear on his way to town. Quite pleased with his fashionable attire he felt he would surely impress everyone.

On the road, he met a crow. The bird challenged the bear's fashion conscience. He told him he had everything wrong. According to the crow, the men were presently wearing frying pan hats, bed linen clothes, and paper bag shoes.

The bear looked at his fine hat, suit, and shoes and headed home to change.

When he returned to town, he was

greeted by laughter and ridicule. He was dressed like a fool. Embarrassed, he turned and ran for home.

On the way he met the crow again. He demanded to know why the crow had tricked him so meanly. The crow calmly responded with a laugh as he flew away, "I told you many things, but I never once said I was telling you the truth." (Adapted from Arnold Lobel's fable *The Bear and the Crow*.)

SIZING IT UP YOURSELF
Have you ever been the victim of a lie? Wanting to believe something so much that you swallowed the hook like the bear did? Then, *WHAM* — ridicule and/or embarrassment.

Have you ever made someone the victim of a lie of yours?

Think about the power of gossip — how we love it. We sometimes start it. Seldom does it concern itself with the truth. Just gets the rumor going. But what about the pain that it causes someone? Dishonesty stings.

When was a time when someone was dishonest with you? Be honest in answering the following questions about that time.

- What were your feelings?
- How did you handle the situation?
- What was the outcome?

Now reverse that question. When was a time when you were dishonest with someone? Ask yourself the following questions.

- What was the situation?
- What happened?
- How did you feel?

CHEATING IS EASY, BUT...

WOW! There are so many ways to be dishonest. Every day in the newspaper you read about dishonesty. You hear it from your friends. You see your teachers get angry about it. You feel the heat from your parents when you practice it. What's the big deal anyway?

Here's the problem: Dishonesty destroys character. No matter what kind—lying, cheating on tests, stealing, gossiping to destroy a friendship—it's all a ZERO.

People don't like cheats. Lying does not win friends. But it's easy. Especially when you don't get caught. Those keep-me-out-of-trouble fibs just dig the hole deeper.

Ever wonder why you don't feel so good inside when you cheat or lie? God knows the motives of your heart. That's God's voice speaking. You are on the wrong path.

You see, God created us special (Psalm 8). Part of God is built into us. Since God is truth (Jesus said, "You shall know the truth, and the truth shall set you free"), anything untruthful hurts us.

Being honest and truthful is hard. If you have friends who are not honest, it is more difficult for you to be. That's why it is important to hang around people who will build your character up and not tear it down.

RELATIONAL HONESTY
Think back to your honesty profile. Write down your score: _____. What did you learn about yourself? What covenant did you make?

Think about all the relationships you have. Here are a few. Give yourself a letter grade from A to E based on the current level of honesty you give that relationship. (A means a high level of honesty; E means things aren't so hot.)

_____ Your parents
_____ Friends
_____ Teachers
_____ Yourself
_____ God
_____ Brothers/Sisters
_____ Friends' parents

SOME PRACTICAL SUGGESTIONS
If you struggle with being honest try some of these hints.

1. Pray for God's help to be more honest. Prayer is powerful.

2. Take the risk of telling the truth in all situations. That leap of faith to tell the truth is scary. Especially if a nice little lie will keep you out of trouble. Funny thing is, the truth is usually less severe than the consequence of a lie.

> I'VE HEARD THAT MOTHS CAN EAT AN ENTIRE SWEATER.

MINDY DENIES ALL KNOWLEDGE OF HER SISTER'S MISSING SWEATER.

3. Talk with your parents about their feelings on honesty. Your parents value honesty. That's why they probably come down on you when you lie. Be open with them. Talk together about ways you can be more truthful.

4. Choose friends who value honesty. If you hang around people who cheat all the time, it will become easier for you to do it too. Select friends who are honest. It will rub off on you.

5. Read what God's Word says about honesty. Try Proverbs 8:7 and 12:17, 19.

A VERY IMPORTANT QUALITY
Remember the bear story! Life is full of dishonest people like the crow. If you want to build Christian character, you must have the quality of truth and honesty. There is no character without it. You will attract people with it.

PETER'S EXPERIENCE
When you do mess up (and we all do) and face the consequence of being dishonest, take it to God. Forgiveness waits. It heals the pain. God's grace is so wonderful.

Peter faced a powerful moment of dishonesty when he denied knowing Jesus (Matthew 26:69-75). Regret over his guilt just about did him in. After the Resurrection, Jesus came to Peter and told him He still loved him. That made all the difference. Peter became the "rock" on which the church was built.

TAKE THE DARE

Draw a bull's eye on a sheet of paper. Circle a big target in the middle. In the center, write one area of dishonesty in your life. For example, you might say, "Not telling my parents the whole truth." Hang it up on the back of your door. Commit to hit the target in the coming week and erase that dishonesty.

ON-THE-JOB TRAINING
CHAPTER TWO

If you were being robbed, would you trust the police to come help you?

If you were in a fire, would you trust the fire department to rescue you and put it out?

If you were having an operation, would you trust the doctors and nurses to take care of you?

If you needed help with math, would you trust your teacher to spend some time with you?

These are just a few situations of trust. Hopefully, you answered yes to all of them. Trust means having confidence in the reliability of a person or thing.

PEOPLE I KNOW
Write down the names of 5 people you trust. Then put one thing that person has done to earn your trust.

PERSON   EARNED TRUST BY:
1.

2.

3.

4.

5.

Trust isn't automatic. We learn to trust others through experience — placing our confidence in them over and over. These five people have earned your trust over time.

TRUST BUSTERS

There are people we trust and people we don't trust. Think of three people you don't trust—and why not.

PERSON	REASON FOR DISTRUST
1.	
2.	
3.	

Maybe each one did something to destroy your trust. Maybe you just don't like that person. Maybe you heard a rumor. Something inside you says, "I don't trust you."

TRUSTWORTHINESS POLL

Now we get to you. What's your trust level? Well, really, how would you rate your reliability when it comes to trust?

Take this trustworthiness poll. Circle Y (Yes) if the statement is always true for you. Circle N (No) if it is never true. Circle M (Maybe) if it is sometimes true.

Y	N	M	I would never betray a friend's secret unless it was a life-threatening situation.
Y	N	M	I complete every task I say I will do.
Y	N	M	I keep my word about being on time.
Y	N	M	If I make a promise, I always keep it.
Y	N	M	I don't try to second guess what other people are thinking.
Y	N	M	I give my family the same commitment I give my friends.
Y	N	M	I believe that God is working in my life.
Y	N	M	I don't take advantage of people for my gain.
Y	N	M	My parents can always trust my word.
Y	N	M	I am honest but not mean when giving someone my opinion.
Y	N	M	I don't tell people what they should do.
Y	N	M	I have the reputation of being very trustworthy.

Add up your Yes, No, and Maybe responses. Then check out the score card below.

YES ____   NO ____   MAYBE ____

Number of Yes answers
9–12 = You are very trustworthy.
6–8 = You are usually trustworthy.
3–5 = You are struggling a bit with being trustworthy.
0–2 = Being trustworthy just isn't your thing.

(Trustworthiness Poll adapted by permission from *Youth and Parents Together*, Mike Gillespie, © 1988, Group, Loveland, Colorado.)

WHAT'S NEXT?

Now that you have a good idea of how trustworthy you are, what can you do?

If you rated high in the poll, then keep striving for that same level of trustworthiness. Obviously you are trying to respond to God's call on your life. Trust is important to you. You are showing others that you have that trait.

If you were disappointed with your score, try these suggestions.

- Decide why you are having trouble being trustworthy.
  ✓ Is it your attitude?
  ✓ Are you hanging around people who don't value trust?
  ✓ Are you trying to get even with your parents?

- Make a commitment to work on trust.
  ✓ Start keeping your word.
  ✓ Don't make a promise you won't honor.
  ✓ Don't betray trust just to get even with someone.
  ✓ Start being more responsible in your behavior.

- Pray about your trust level.
- ✓ Ask God to help you be more trustworthy.
- ✓ Tell God your struggles with trust.
- ✓ Depend on God to empower you to be more trustworthy.

TAKE THE DARE

Take a calendar. For one month, take the dare to keep your word about everything. Don't make a promise you won't keep. If you tell someone you will do something, then follow through. Each day you are successful, put a check mark on that day. Be faithful in the simple tasks.

When the month is over and you see all those check marks, you will be on your way to greater levels of trustworthiness.

Read Luke 19:11-27. What can you learn from Jesus about being trustworthy?

A TRUE TEST OF CHARACTER
CHAPTER THREE

Sharon's voice echoes clear to the end of the hall. She's screaming at her friend (ex-friend) Lisa. "I'll never forgive you—never, never, never! I told you not to tell anyone I like Craig. Now it's all over the school."

WHAT'S ALL THE FUSS?
Sharon is caught in the forgiveness trap. She has decided to punish someone out of anger.

Would you tell Sharon to forgive and forget? Why or why not?

WHAT'S YOUR OPINION?
What do you think about the level of forgiveness in your life? Is that a character trait that someone would identify in you?

When was the last time you forgave someone? When was the last time you received forgiveness from someone? Is there someone in your life you refuse to forgive? Is there someone who refuses to forgive you?

Those are tough questions. But they must be answered if you are to grow in forgiveness.

CONDITIONAL FORGIVENESS
Most of the time we get by on conditional forgiveness. You know. The kind where you say the words or go through the motions. Do you really mean it, though, when you go about it like that? No!

Some of the conditions we put on forgiveness are as follows:

- "Say you're sorry first."
- "I want to hear one more time that you didn't mean it."
- "I'm going to hold this grudge awhile, thank you."
- "I'm not in a forgiving mood today."

When we put conditions on forgiveness, though, we set ourselves up as God. We decide that we are going to make the rules. That's dangerous.

God built into each of us the capacity to forgive. It is the very essence of God's personality.

FORGIVENESS BARRIERS
Did you ever wonder what makes forgiveness difficult for you? It's those luring forgiveness barriers. They also keep others from being able to forgive a wrong you have done.

Some of the more common barriers are:

- GRUDGES — Jane is angry with Susan for stealing her boyfriend. She's going to hold a grudge against her the entire school year.

- GETTING EVEN — Kenny is still upset because Tatia told Paula he likes her. He decides to start a rumor that Tatia is in love with John — a guy at school no one likes.

- HATE — Kim cannot forgive her father for the divorce. She hates him so much for breaking up the family. She never wants to speak to him again.

Are these barriers to forgiveness in your life?

CHRISTIAN FORGIVENESS

God gives us permission to embrace the Christian character trait of forgiveness. We are called by Jesus' example to be forgivers.

Think about Jesus' life. What do you remember about His style of forgiving? When He found someone doing wrong He didn't shut that person out. Read John 7:53–8:11. He said, "Go and leave your life of sin" (v. 11). His for giveness opened the door to life.

Your ability to forgive someone can open the same door for them.

WHERE DO YOU STAND?
Well, how do you think you would grade yourself on forgiveness?

A. I give and receive forgiveness freely. I am sincere when I forgive. I don't hold grudges, hate, or try to get even. I admit when I have wronged others and seek out their forgiveness.

B. I give and receive forgiveness well. I am sincere but may be prone to grudges or get even tactics. It's hard for me to tell someone I'm sorry. But eventually I get around to it.

C. I'm pretty average on forgiveness. I can hold a pretty strong grudge. I've come up with some great get-even tricks. I can't always say I'm sorry for my mistakes that hurt others.

D. I'm struggling with forgiveness. I know so many people I can't forgive right now. I don't want to let go of my anger. I'm afraid to do that. It's very hard to say, "I'm sorry" to people.

F. I flunk out! Forgiveness is not my thing. I enjoy grudges, little hates, and wonderful get-evens. I'll never say, "I'm sorry" to anyone about anything. Forgiveness stinks.

Did you find yourself somewhere on that scale? Everyone is there. Being honest about it is tough. Remember the character trait of honesty?

FORGIVENESS FORMULA

If you need help getting your forgiveness act together, try this formula.

1. Recognize the need to forgive or receive forgiveness — Own up to the fact that you or someone in your life needs forgiveness.
2. Identify your feelings — It's OK to have strong feelings when you feel wronged. What you do with those feelings is another matter, though.
3. Identify the barriers — Is there a barrier to forgiveness? Are you holding a grudge? Do you want to get even? Are you being consumed by hate? Are you angry with yourself?
4. Go to God — Forgiveness will never happen until you turn it over to God. At that point, the process of healing begins.
5. Go to the person — If you have wronged someone, then ask to be forgiven. If someone has wronged you, then go to the person and let him or her know you want to help set things right.
6. Let go of it — You've forgiven or been forgiven. Now let go of it. Get on with your life. Look for the sunshine.

7. Remember, forgiveness takes time — Even though you have done steps 1–6 you will still need time. Be patient with yourself and allow God to work.

TAKE THE DARE

Identify someone in your life whom you need to forgive. Write that person's name on a sheet of paper and tape it to your mirror. Begin the 7 steps to forgiveness.

Read about some other people who messed up. God's history with us is one of forgiveness. That's what Jesus said as He died for us. "Father, forgive them, for they know not what they do."

Check out David's big goof and his need for forgiveness (2 Samuel 11–12) and Paul's word to the Colossians about forgiveness (Colossians 3:13).

RISKING YOUR LIFE OVER RESPECT
CHAPTER FOUR

Would you...
- Have respect for a friend who continually used vulgar words?
- Have respect for a teacher who always called your class the school dummies?
- Have respect for a parent who lectured you about not drinking but then came home drunk?
- Have respect for a coach who talked about sportsmanship but then blew up during games?
- Have respect for yourself if you never took a stand for something you valued?
- Have respect for a government official caught using drugs?

I doubt it. Respect has to be earned. It is not automatic.

WHOM DO YOU RESPECT?
Identify people in your life you respect.
- An adult you hold in high regard. _____
- A teacher at school. _____
- A classmate who is not a close friend. _____
- A person in the Bible who lived up to his or her faith. _____
- A friend. _____
- A friend's parent. _____
- A government official. _____

Was that an easy list to complete? You may have found out that you are not quite sure who it is you respect. That's been happening a lot in our society.

EARNING RESPECT
Have you ever stopped to think what a person has to do to earn your respect? What's the answer?

Complete this sentence: "To earn my respect a person would have to _____."

Let's reverse that. What would you have to do to earn the respect of another person. "To earn respect of another, I have to _____."

Which was easier to complete? Probably the one where you listed what a person should do to earn *your* respect.

WHAT'S YOUR OPINION?
Look at the statements below and follow the instructions. They will help you sort out some of your opinions about respect. Circle A or B.

1. When it comes to respecting my parents I...
   A. Respect them a lot.
   B. Respect them very little.
2. I respect my friends...
   A. All the time.
   B. Most of the time.
3. My friends respect me...
   A. All the time.
   B. Most of the time.

Rank your choices—1 = Top choice; 2 = Second choice; 3 = Third choice.

4. Respect for God means:
   _____ Caring for creation.
   _____ Going to church every Sunday.
   _____ Saying kind things to others.
5. My family could use more respect when it comes to:
   _____ The way we talk to one another.
   _____ Our attitudes toward one another.
   _____ The level of concern and patience we give one another.
6. I need to be more respectful to:
   _____ My friends.
   _____ My teachers.
   _____ Myself.
7. Giving respect means:
   _____ Not getting my way all the time.
   _____ Not talking back to adults.
   _____ Not using sarcasm.

DISRESPECT GAME

There's a new game available. It's called the Disrespect Game. It's a top seller. Check out the directions.

DIRECTIONS:
1. Pick your team.
2. Decide on ways to put down and ridicule all the other players.
3. Play dirty.
4. Don't worry if someone gets hurt.
5. Talk back. Use sarcasm. Be irresponsible.
6. You win when you make someone angry or get them to cry.

Would you like that game? It sounds like pretty scary stuff. But actually we play it all the time. We play it with our friends, with our parents, with our teachers, and even with ourselves.

It's a painful game. And it hurts.

Remember how you felt the last time someone was disrespectful to you? That's how it feels when it comes from you.

Have you played that game with your parents or teachers? What response did you get? (Not a free banana split coupon for sure.) Parents are hurt by disrespect too. The more you use it the more destructive the battle.

But you deserve respect as well. Ever feel like your parents don't respect you? Lots of young teens do. It's painful, particularly when you feel you haven't done anything to earn their disrespect.

BUILDING RESPECT

An important character trait of the Christian is respect. If we are to be Christ's disciples, we must share respect.

Here are some positive ways to build respect with others.

BUILDING-RESPECT LIST
You build respect when you . . .
- Listen to others.
- Stand up for your faith.
- Stamp out gossip.
- Use kind and caring words.
- Are a loyal and faithful friend.
- Have strong values.
- Respond lovingly to your family.

- Protect God's creation.
- Worship and study God's Word.
- Let God's Holy Spirit work in your life.
- Support and honor teachers.
- Obey laws.
- Keep your promises and commitments.

That's just a beginning list. All of those things help build respect. You must be willing to practice them if you are to have the character trait of respect.

WHERE DO YOU NEED HELP?

Where is your respect level? Do your friends, parents, teachers, and God see you as a respectful person? Or do they see you as someone who plays the Disrespect Game?

Building respect takes work. Hard work. And it can be wiped out in one bad decision. Keep working to build respect.

You can find help in the Bible as you strive to build respect. Peter knew how important it was for members of the early church to respect one another. In 1 Peter 2:17 he tells us to show proper respect to everyone.

TAKE THE DARE
Write out the letters to the word RESPECT on a sheet of paper. Write one sentence beginning with each letter that says something you will do to show respect. For example, you might put for R: Regard every person as special in God's eyes.

When you finish, stick it on your door. Remind yourself each day to show respect. Showing respect earns respect.

DOUBLE DARE: Think about your parents. Where do you have trouble on the respect scale? Decide on one specific step you will take to raise your respect level. For example, you might decide to stop using sarcasm.

STANDING ALONE
CHAPTER FIVE

PART 2: THE POWER OF MOTIVATION

The group opened the door carefully as the last person arrived. "Lock it!" shouted a loud voice from the back of the room. "We're all here now."

The evening was like any other. They shared a meal and sang songs of praise. The room was filled with the Holy Spirit.

They talked about their lives and struggles. A lot of time was spent in prayer for one another. Scripture seemed to come alive as they read Mark's Gospel.

Discussion was lively. It focused on

the story about the sower. Some in the group were growing crops. Rain had been scarce. They related to the seed being choked by weeds or shallow soil.

Suddenly, without warning, the dreaded pounding at the door. "Open up now or we will break it down!"

There was no escape. Nowhere to run or hide. They had known the risk. And they had taken it anyway. It was the only way of life worthwhile.

The door crashed open. Armor-clad Roman soldiers stormed the room. Men, women, and children were yanked up and dragged away. There was no mercy. Jail and death awaited.

As they were being beaten and tied together, a neighbor stood watching in a doorway. A Roman soldier paid him several pieces of silver.

CHRISTIAN COURAGE
What's your reaction to that story? Is it fact or fiction? Could it have happened or did it happen?

Courage is the ability to trust that God is with you regardless of the circumstance. The early church had courage. People defied Roman decrees and met secretly. Sometimes they were caught. They were executed. All because they made the commitment to follow a man called Jesus.

The story was real. It happened.

WHAT IF?
What if you faced a similar situation like the early church? What if you had to pay a price for your faith? What if it really took courage to be a Christian? Would you have that courage? Try these "what ifs" on for size.

WHAT IF . . .
- You had to move to a new school and make new friends?
- You were told you had cancer and had only one year to live?
- You had no home and lived on the street every day?
- You couldn't be a member of your church unless you came every week?
- You were hated at your school be

cause you wouldn't cheat?
- You were rejected by your peer group because you wouldn't drink with them?

Do you have the character trait of courage that could meet these challenges? Would you overcome them or would they overcome you? As a Christian you must develop the character trait of courage if you are to grow.

What would you risk on faith? What would you give up, let go of, stand firm on, or face persecution over if your faith depended on it?

Think about your life up to this moment. Draw a symbol to represent something from your past.

- A time when you faced a family crisis that took courage.
- A time when you faced ridicule because of your values.
- A time when you went through a tough crisis with a friend.
- A time when it took courage to survive the school year.

If you have faced these, you know know what it means to have courage.

You know what it means to stand alone, to feel like everyone has abandoned you. Yet, God was there, waiting and hoping you would turn to Him.

A LEAP OF FAITH
Courage becomes a character trait only at the moment when you take a leap of faith, when you decide to trust God to get you through a risky situation.

Where is your courage level? Not the courage to take on stupid challenges like TP'ing a house. Courage to take risks of faith. Risks like . . .
- Standing up for a friend being the brunt of gossip.
- Changing your lifestyle to conserve the world's resources.
- Controlling your sexual desires.
- Saying no to alcohol and other drugs.
- Telling your parents the truth, even if you know you'll be punished.

Do you remember Daniel? A man in the Old Testament. He had strong faith and prayed every morning. A law was passed forbidding prayer to anyone but the king. The penalty was death.

People watched to see what Daniel would do. He still prayed. He was arrested and sentenced to death in a den of lions (Daniel 6). God was with him and he was never harmed.

That took courage. Do you have the courage to risk your life like Daniel risked his?

THE COURAGE CHALLENGE

Try these challenges to be more courageous in living out your faith.

- **C** Care about unpopular people at school.
- **O** Organize a group to start a recycling project.
- **U** Urge your friends to stop gossiping.
- **R** Read your Bible and pray daily.
- **A** Accept Jesus Christ as your Lord and Savior.
- **G** Go and help someone in trouble.
- **E** Encourage better communication with your parents.

Now, make your own list.

C

O

U

R

A

G

E

ADVICE FROM PAUL
The Apostle Paul learned a lot about courage. He faced constant ridicule for spreading the Gospel. In his letter to the Corinthians he told us what he had gone through (2 Corinthians 11:23-27).

Paul faced . . .
- Shipwreck.
- Being beaten with rods.
- Being whipped.
- Being stoned.
- Being chased by bandits.

- Jail.
- Sleepless nights.
- Hunger and thirst.

Hey, these wouldn't make your top ten list any time soon. (Except maybe the sleepless nights.)

Later, Paul told his secret of endurance. Read it in Philippians 4:10-13.

Paul's secret was: _____

TAKE THE DARE
Now it's time to get personal. Where do you face a challenge of courage? Write the words SCHOOL, FRIENDSHIP, FAMILY, and GOD on separate sheets of paper. Put them in a sack. Shake it and pull one out. Now, complete the rest of the DARE.

Dear God: You know the situation I face. You know I need courage to _____. I ask You now for that courage.

45

JUST WAIT A LITTLE WHILE LONGER
CHAPTER SIX

John's dad was walking by his room. He heard the model car John was building slam into the bottom of the trash can. It busted into broken pieces. John's voice told it all. "I'm so mad at that stupid car! I've worked on it for three nights and can't get it together. I've had it." His dad said calmly, "Sounds like you just ran out of patience, Son."

Susan had been helping her little sister Beth with math for 30 minutes. Finally, she yelled through the house, "Mother, I quit. Beth just doesn't understand. I have no more patience for this."

OPENING THE DOOR

What were those situations about? That's right. They dealt with patience. Guess you're saying to yourself, *Oh boy, here we go with the "Why don't you have more patience?" routine.*

Wrong. But you will read some things that will help you decide where patience fits into your life.

ANY RESEMBLANCE?

Hey, are you one of those characters?
- Are you a JOHN TYPE who loses patience with himself and destroys his hard work?
- Are you a SUSAN TYPE who goes for a while then says "So long" when the person doesn't come through for her?

Patience is hard. It takes practice. It doesn't come easy. What tries your patience?

Ever hear the phrase, That tries my patience; or, You try my patience so much? Have you said one? Most of us have, at some time or another. We get into a situation where our patience doesn't even have a chance. We get involved helping someone and our patience fades fast.

Let's do a quick survey. Here are three areas where you spend a lot of time. Under each one, write something that happens to you there that *tries* your patience. You know, stuff that sends you up a wall. Like "At school I get so impatient with teachers who give me junk work just to fill time."

- AT HOME—

- AT SCHOOL—

- AT CHURCH—

You probably came up with those pretty quickly. *You* know what drives you crazy. Trouble is, you might not recognize how your impatience affects others. Impatience is a normal part of our lives. We just need to know how to deal with it.

PATIENCE AND GOD
Patience is an important character trait for a Christian. It is a gift from God. That's right. Patience is a gift from God. It's something we have to work on, develop, try hard at. Is that true about you? Does patience come easy for you, or is it a constant battle?

ADVICE FROM JESUS
Ever think about how much patience Jesus had? Just imagine if everywhere you went, you were mobbed. People wanting to be blessed, people wanting to be healed, people with questions about God, people wanting to get rid of you.

Once a large group was listening to Him. He told them many things about God that day. One thing He talked about was patience. Jesus told the crowd not to be so impatient about tomorrow—about all the stuff of their lives. Enjoy the moment and trust God to be with you (see Matthew 6:25-34).

Patience was part of Jesus' strength.

That's why he could handle sarcasm, deal with obnoxious people, answer questions skillfully, heal, and — probably the most challenging — train His disciples.

SEEKING PATIENCE

What are some steps you can take to be a more patient person? Try these on for size.

1. **Put your mind in gear before you engage your mouth.**
- Don't always be so quick to respond. Think about the power of your words. Are they building up or tearing down? Jesus always used words that built people up. Thinking before speaking can help your patience level.

2. **Set realistic goals for yourself.**
- Remember John's impatience with his model car? Maybe he picked out one he wasn't ready to tackle. Maybe he should have worked on other cars less complicated first. Then his patience level would be ready for the challenge of a tough model.

- When you set goals, don't reach for the stars right away. They will still be there next year. Know your limits. Yes, challenge yourself, but don't be stupid. If your best time in track is 2 minutes, don't expect to cut it to 1:30 overnight. Try for a 1:55 first. Go from there.

3. **Don't try to do it alone — ask for help.**

- Jesus told people to be patient with themselves. Ask God to work in your life. Identify the areas of your impatience and turn them over to God.
- Take the challenge to improve. If you never finish a conversation with your parents then make a commitment to do it once. That's the starting point. If you have no patience with math, find a friend to work with you. That's a starting place. You can identify lots more of these.

4. Practice, practice, practice.
- Patience doesn't happen without practice.

5. Worry less about the things you cannot control.
- Often your impatience centers on things you cannot control. Learn to identify those areas. Life is not always fair. Feelings, attitudes, and actions of others are beyond your control. Accept that.
- Here's some advice: "Lord, help me change the things I can, accept the things I cannot, and have the wisdom to know the difference." Write that on a sheet of paper and put it up in your room.

PATIENCE AWARD

Let's look at the good news of patience in your life. Where are you strongest? Give yourself an award.

In the trophy below, write the area where you have the greatest patience. For example, you might say, "I have great patience when it comes to finishing my homework" or "I have great patience when it comes to practicing the piano." Fill in the trophy. Congratulations! You're working toward the character trait of patience.

TAKE THE DARE
This week, tackle one area of impatience in your life. Set a specific goal to do that. Here's how.

Take a sheet of paper and write out what you want to accomplish. For example, you could say you want to be more patient with your math teacher.

Tape the sheet to the wall. Each night tear off a piece of that paper if you worked on that goal and made progress. At the end of the week check how much is still there. Try it.

IT'S GOING TO TAKE MORE THAN LEGO BLOCKS
CHAPTER SEVEN

In the last chapter we talked about patience. Here's another P word: Perseverance. It's just as tough as patience.

Did you ever have one of those days when you were ready to give up? Wanted to throw in the towel? Chuck it all?

Not doing that is what perseverance is all about. You might call it stick-to-itiveness. It's closely related to patience, but you need patience first before you can have perseverance.

Are you a persevere-er? How would you handle the following situations?

PERSEVERE AT PLAY PRACTICE?

Play practice was in its final week. Jean had the lead part. The rest of the cast had memorized their lines but Jean had not. Every practice was becoming a struggle. People were getting angry. Finally, two days before the performance, Jean quit. She told the others, "I can't learn these stupid lines. I can't. It's just too hard for me."

- What would you have thought if you were in the play?
- What do you think was Jean's problem?
- How could Jean improve her character skill of perseverance?
- When have you felt a little like Jean?

PERSEVERE IN PIANO PLAYING?

Karen came up with every excuse possible when it came time for piano practice. But she loved the lesson with Mrs. Roberts. She liked hearing, "You have special talent, Karen." Her daily practice sessions were a different story, though. Karen's mom was constantly after her to sit at the piano. But then, she only gave it a half-hearted effort—just to get it over with and keep her mother off her case.

One week Mrs. Roberts said, "Karen, I'm dropping you as one of my students. I need to make a place for someone else. You have great talent but our time together has been a waste. It's obvious to me that you never practice. That was the deal we made when you started six months ago. I'm sorry. I've made my decision and your parents agree."

Karen was crushed. She needed the affirmation she got during her lessons. She just couldn't understand why Mrs. Roberts made that decision.
- What was Karen's problem?
- What might have been some reasons she couldn't follow through with the practice?
- When have you been in a similar situation?
- What kind of perseverance did Karen need?
- How do you feel about her wasting her talent?

PERSEVERE WITH PARTYING PALS?

Ralph couldn't take it any more. It was his friend Jim. They had been buddies a long time. But lately Jim had been acting like a real jerk. Ralph couldn't figure.

It began at the party when Jim started using dirty language. Then he started saying mean things to people at school. And his good-student status dropped — he got nothing but D's now. Ralph tried, but he couldn't get Jim to talk about it.

One day, as the two friends walked out of school together, Ralph said, "Jim, I don't understand you anymore. You're doing stupid things. And you won't talk to me. It's almost become impossible to be your friend."

Jim turned on him in anger. "Thanks a lot, loser! And for your information, we never were friends anyway. Just because we've known each other for five years doesn't mean anything. I don't need you and I never did. I don't need anybody, so you can just get lost!"

Ralph walked away, hurt and confused. Jim turned in the other direction. Tears ran down his face.

When Jim got home, his dad was just getting out of bed. "Hey son, get me a beer. NOW! And start supper for your mother. What are you waiting for? Get to it, boy!"

- What was going on between Ralph and Jim?
- What did Ralph need to do to keep the friendship going?
- What did Jim need to do?
- Who was at fault?
- Ralph persevered in his friendship with Jim for quite some time. Should he keep at it?
- Why had Jim changed? Could the need for perseverance apply in his case?
- When was a time you faced a situation like this?

PROBING FOR PERSEVERANCE

Check out the following questions. Think about your perseverance level — your stick-to-itiveness.

How long would you last or survive or endure...
- a vacation with your family? _____ days
- daily homework? _____ hours (Be optimistic.)
- being grounded from seeing your friends? _____ days
- not being able to talk on the telephone? _____ days
- hard, strenuous exercise? _____ minutes
- reading Scripture? _____ minutes
- sticking by a friend? _____ (You set it.)
- sitting in a worship service? _____ hours/minutes
- a conversation with your parents? _____ hours/minutes
- praying to God? _____ minutes
- not being allowed to go to church or youth group? _____ (You set it.)

GOD'S PROMISES

Perseverance, like patience, is strengthened when we rely on God. Check out these promises. Read:
- Psalm 27:1; Psalm 121 — God promises us protection.

- Psalm 18:30-33 — God promises us strength.
- Psalm 103:1-18 — God promises us forgiveness.
- Psalm 119:1-5 — God promises us guidance.
- Psalm 46:1-3; 91:1-6 — God promises us safety.
- Psalm 139:1-6 — God promises us His presence.

Do you realize what we have? PROTECTION. STRENGTH. FORGIVENESS. GUIDANCE. SAFETY. PRESENCE. Those are some promises!

Knowing that God is behind you like that makes it a little easier to persevere.

MAKING IT PERSONAL
The 23rd Psalm is powerful. It could easily be your theme song for your persevering. In the blanks below, write your first name. Then go back and read the psalm.

The Lord is _____ shepherd, _____ shall not be in want. He makes _____ lie down in green pastures, He leads _____ beside quiet waters, He restores _____ soul. He guides _____ in paths of righteousness for His name's sake. Even though _____ walks through the valley of the shadow of death, _____ will fear no evil, for You are with _____; Your rod and your staff they comfort _____. You prepare a table before _____ in the presence of _____ enemies. You anoint _____ head with oil; _____ cup overflows. Surely goodness and love will follow _____ all the days of _____ life, and _____ will dwell in the house of the Lord forever.

TAKE THE DARE

Well, how would you rate your perseverance level? Do you have the Christian character trait of stick-to-itiveness?

Try this challenge. Get a 1,000-piece jigsaw puzzle. Start working on it even if you hate puzzles. When you get done, you will be able to shout "I PERSEVERED!"

THOSE GRUMBLING HEBREWS
CHAPTER EIGHT

A long time ago, God chose the Hebrews. They were to be a great nation and bless all the people of the earth. God took them out of slavery in Egypt. He promised them their own land. Moses was their leader. But even with God on their side, they were a stubborn and discontented people. All they wanted to do was complain.

- "We're thirsty. Where's the water, Moses?"
- "We're hungry. Where's the food, Moses?"
- "We're tired. Let's quit walking, Moses."
- "We're afraid. How are you going to

protect us, Moses?"
- "Where are you, Moses? Let's make a new God."
- "We can't conquer that new land. You're stupid, Moses."

On and on they whined and whined. Sometimes when God talked through Moses, they would be OK for a few days. But then it was soon back to the whining.

What would you do with a family like that? Would you survive? Would you have been one of the whiners? The problem was the Hebrews had little self-control.

YOUR RESISTANCE LEVEL

Self-control is an important character trait for Christians. Without it we have no discipline.

Do you get angry when your parents discipline you? Even when you knew the consequence of your action beforehand? That's a sign you are struggling with self-control. Self-control is the ability to resist life's temptations. It is the ability to have patience and perseverance.

Look at the list below. It's filled with things that tempt your self-control. Rate yourself a 1 if you have no control in that area; a 2 if you have some control; and a 3 if you have lots of control.

_____ Yelling at your parents
_____ Sneaking a drink
_____ Smoking
_____ Cheating
_____ Starting gossip or passing it on
_____ Sexual desires
_____ Fighting with brothers/sisters
_____ Conserving our earth's resources
_____ Telling the truth
_____ Using friends for your own gain
_____ Being stubborn about everything
_____ Respecting adults
_____ Using profanity
_____ Overeating
_____ Spending money
_____ Belonging to cliques

What numbers did you put? Were you honest about it? Understanding where you need self-control is the first step to change. What would be your overall self-control rating—a 1, 2, or 3?

PUSHING THE WRONG BUTTONS

Did you know you have control buttons? They're things that people do that spin you out of control. That's what people mean when they say you got your button pushed.

What get's you going? What really ticks you off and makes you mad? What makes you lose control? Put a yes or no beside each sentence below.

I LOSE CONTROL...
- _____ when someone doesn't get my name right.
- _____ when my parents keep asking me, "Why?"
- _____ when I'm around my bratty brothers/sisters.
- _____ when teachers single me out.
- _____ when I see someone being hurt.
- _____ when I see animals mistreated.
- _____ when God doesn't answer my prayer.

_____ when my friends ignore me.
_____ if I'm laughed at.
_____ if things don't go my way.
_____ when my parents ground me.
_____ when someone tells a secret of mine.
_____ when no one listens to me.

These are just a sample of things that might push your control button. Make a list of others that come to mind so you can always be aware of them. Try to work on these.

SECRETS OF SELF-CONTROL

Here are some tips for staying in control.

1. Separate the deed from the doer. Can you separate actions from the person? God doesn't expect you to like the wrong done to you. He does expect you, though, to still love the person who did it. That's tough. But don't you want the same treatment?

2. Look for the good in others. Do you look for the good in others first?

Or do you always notice their flaws ... nicks ... wart ... blemishes? If you notice the bad first, it will erode your self-control.

3. Pray for self-control. How do you rate on prayer? Have you discovered the power of God's Holy Spirit to help your self-control? Go to God in prayer. Ask for help with your self-control. Seek out the power of the Holy Spirit to work in your life.

4. Say no to life's temptations. Do you know the temptations you face? Do you wrestle inside with those competing voices of "yes" and "no"? They'll never stop. But you will find help in self-control to follow the advice of your "no" voice.

TAKE THE DARE
Read Psalm 119:33-35. Look back at the 1s or 2s you put on your survey. Write each one on a sheet of paper. Tape them in a row on your wall. Each day you show self-control over one of those areas, put a big X through it. See how long it takes to do them all.

PART 3: BUILDING SPIRITUAL MUSCLES

A VERY SPECIAL WOMAN
CHAPTER NINE

The story is told of a very special woman. She married into a family of two brothers. It was a kind and loving family. And God was the center of their family life.

This woman didn't know God, though. She worshiped several gods who were very different from the true God.

Tragedy struck. The woman's father-in-law died. Later her husband and his brother both died. Now there were three widows. The mother told her daughters-in-law to go back to their own families. She said they would be better off there.

One went back. One didn't. Our special woman stayed with her mother-in-law. She made a lifelong commitment to her and accepted her God. She would follow her mother-in-law wherever she went.

This special woman was a very hard worker. She was seen in the field gathering grain. A kind man owned the field and offered to protect her. Later, she married this man. Her name was Ruth. She became the great-grandmother to King David. Her life story is in the Book of Ruth.

Ruth is a wonderful example of the character trait of faithfulness.

FAITHFUL RELATIONSHIPS

What makes a faithful friend? The kind of special person you would trust with every secret. They're hard to find. They get the revered title of BEST FRIEND.

Think about your best friends. Most of us have 1–3 best friends. How do they show their faithfulness? What characteristics do you appreciate most about each of them? Write those down.

BEST FRIEND #1: _____
   I appreciate his/her qualities of:
A. _____
B. _____
C. _____
D. _____

BEST FRIEND #2: _____
   I appreciate his/her qualities of:
A. _____
B. _____
C. _____
D. _____

BEST FRIEND #3: _____
   I appreciate his/her qualities of:
A. _____
B. _____
B. _____
C. _____

FAMILY FAITHFULNESS
Families are another place where faithfulness is important. Think about your family. What characteristics do

you appreciate about one another? Kindness, caring, listening, laughter, or patience may be some.

Fill in this FAMILY CREST.

- What one fruit of the Spirit would you give each family member? (Check Galatians 5:22 for ideas.)
- Draw a symbol to represent each family member.
- Which of these three words would you give each family member: Faith, hope, or love?
- Write a specific act that each member shares to show faithfulness to the family.
- Do you now affirm that your family

is important? How do you rate your faithfulness toward your family?

Think about these questions.
- Am I caring and loving toward family members?
- Am I patient with family members?
- Am I supportive of my family?

These are ways to demonstrate your character trait of faithfulness.

FAITHFULNESS TO GOD

We've talked about friends and family. Now let's look at God. How would God evaluate your faithfulness to Him? To His Word? Check the items below that you are doing.
- ( ) Attending worship regularly.
- ( ) Being a faithful member of my youth group.
- ( ) Reading my Bible daily.
- ( ) Being faithful in prayer.
- ( ) Relying on God's Holy Spirit.
- ( ) Inviting others to know Jesus Christ.
- ( ) Living out my faith in everything I do.
- ( ) Respecting my parents.

Ever wonder what God thinks about individual Christians? That's a scary question. But the answer will more than please you if you're his child. Read Romans 8:28, 38-39.

What did you find? Isn't it awesome to know that God wants to work for good in your life? If you know God, you understand the character trait of faithfulness.

What great promise did you find in those verses? Read them again. Nothing in all creation can separate God's children from His love in Jesus Christ.

That's the bottom line. The victory. The hope. The fuel for your faithfulness.

BEING MORE FAITHFUL

Now's the time to think about your life. What do you need to do to strengthen your character trait of faithfulness? What can you do to be more faithful in your friendships to others? What can you do to be a more faithful student at your school?

What can you do to be a more faithful member of your family? What can you do to be a more faithful member of your community? What can you do to be a more faithful member of your church?

TAKE THE DARE
Read Psalm 8. Each morning this week, begin your day with that psalm. Go through the day knowing that you were created just a little lower than the angels. You were made in God's image!

How can you faithfully reflect that image?

WALKING ON HOLY GROUND
CHAPTER TEN

It was a normal afternoon. Nothing special going on. The sheep were grazing on the hillside. Moses thought how good his life had been.

Suddenly a strange glow caught his attention. There, up on the mountainside. It looked like a bush was burning. Moses watched with interest. The bush kept burning and burning and wouldn't stop.

The climb was difficult. Jagged rocks. But he was just too curious to let it be. Still he made his way upward. As he got closer, he could see the bush was on fire, but it wasn't burning up. He wondered if he should move any closer. The air was heavy. Like nothing he had ever felt before.

Then that voice. It called his name. "Moses. Moses!" the bush called. Moses felt knots in his stomach. His mouth was dry. His muscles tensed. He couldn't move. All he could do was say, "Here I am."

"Don't come any closer. Take off your sandals. You are standing on holy ground."

As Moses slowly bent down and untied them, his hands probably shook.

"I am the God of your fathers, the God of Abraham, the God of Isaac, and the God of Jacob."

Moses turned away and hid his face in fear. Suddenly, he knew he was in the presence of God (Exodus 3).

What if that had been you instead of Moses? What if God had singled you out to stand before the burning bush?
- Would you have run?
- Would you have made jokes... laughed... paid no attention?

- Would you have been so afraid that your whole body would have shaken?
- Would you have spoken back?
- Would you have taken off your shoes?

Sure, you say, that's just a nice story in the Old Testament. I wasn't there, so I don't have to worry about what might have been.

Wait a minute! You *are* on holy ground. You are in the presence of God.

TOMORROW...

You're at school. Five minutes before third period. You watch the goons across the hall ripping on a short kid. Jokes—put-downs—humiliation. You just stand there and watch. Did you forget? That's holy ground.

You're at home. Your mom tells you supper will be ready in five minutes. Your dad walks into the kitchen and slumps at the table. You keep watching television.

"The company is phasing out my department. I won't have a job in two months," he says to your mom. You hear her say, "Oh, Mark, what are we going to do?" You just keep watching television. Did you forget you are on holy ground?

It's Sunday morning. You grab your best friend and head for the back row. During worship you talk about last night's party. People around you seem annoyed but you don't care. Worship is boring anyway. Have you forgotten you are on holy ground?

YOU ARE THERE

You are on holy ground. Wonder how that can be? You face an opportunity to show reverence every day. Reverence is a deep respect in your heart for God.

Moses experienced a deep reverence for God, and from that day on he tried to do things God's way, not his own way. A Christian must also have that character trait. Every word you say. Every action you do. Every thought you possess can be an act of reverence.

When you are in the halls at school, you are in God's presence. Do you have the courage to stop a put-down?

When you are at home, you are in God's presence. Do you have the courage to react lovingly to your parents?

When you are at church, you are in God's presence. Do you have the courage to worship with excitement?

TAKE THE DARE
Are you a reverent person? It isn't about church. It's about the burning bush—about meeting God and responding to His presence.

Write BE REVERENT in big letters on a long sheet of paper. Tape it on the ceiling above your bed. Each night when you lie there, read it.

Let God work in your life to make you more reverent. Then, watch out! Reverence is contagious. You just might start a wonderful new disease.

LOPSIDED ODDS
CHAPTER ELEVEN

Suppose you were just made commander of an army. The enemy was ready to attack you. How would you prepare? Here's the situation:
- The other army has thousands of soldiers. How many soldiers do you need?
- The other army is camped near you. They will attack soon. How will you defeat them?
- The other army has trained military leaders. You are an average person with no military training. What will you do?

Do those odds sound good to you? Keep reading.

It's about 1050 B.C.—the time of the Judges. Gideon has been called by God to lead the Hebrews. Trouble has come because the neighboring Midianites want to attack them (Judges 6:33–7:22). Thousands of the enemy are camped nearby. They have weapons of death and destruction.

Gideon organizes the Hebrews to respond. A full 32,000 men volunteer. (Now things sound better, don't they?)

Now God enters the situation. The Lord tells Gideon he has too many men. (What?)

Gideon is told to send home any man who is "trembling with fear" over the battle. Guess how many jump ship? Twenty-two thousand. That's right. Twenty-two thousand!

Gideon is left with 10,000 men in his army. God speaks again. He tells Gideon to take them to a stream and let them drink water with their hands. (Can you imagine 10,000 people lined up along a stream?)

Those that lap water from their hands are singled out. Those that kneel and drink with their tongues like dogs are told to go home. After this, the army numbers 300. Can you believe it? Three hundred men against an army of thousands.

But wait! There's more.

God tells Gideon to arm the men with trumpets, torches, and empty jars. (Would you want to fight with those weapons? Probably not.) The men sneak up on the sleeping army and surround the camp. On Gideon's signal they blow the trumpets, smash the jars, and wave their torches in the air.

Now, imagine what you would do if you were awakened like that. Fear runs through the Midianite camp. And chaos. Absolute chaos. The Midianite army thinks they are being attacked by thousands. They end up killing each other.

What a victory! By God's design.

Was Gideon stupid for listening to God? Stupid for going into battle against such terrible odds? Stupid for arming himself with torches, jars, and trumpets?

He may have seemed stupid at first. But he won! This happened because he was obedient to God.

Though he must have had his doubts, he knew it was God's battle to win. Not the Hebrews' battle to win. Not Gideon's to win.

STRUGGLES WITH OBEDIENCE

Obedience is a hard word to swallow. It gets stuck on the way down. It's like trying to digest cotton.

When have you struggled with obedience? Have there been times when obeying the smallest thing sounded harder than hopping up Mt. Everest on one foot?

There's something inside each of us that wants to disobey. A little voice whispering, "You don't have to do that." (Remember Adam and Eve's blunder?)

How's your obedience level? Draw a happy face where you can easily obey.

Draw a stubborn face where you know you sometimes don't obey. (Watch out—it's tricky.)

_____ A teacher who gives homework every night.

_____ A friend who demands a lot of time.

_____ A coach who pushes you really hard.

_____ A parent who tells you to clean your room.

_____ A friend who asks you to skip class.

_____ The lure to try alcohol.

_____ The temptation to have sex.

_____ The impulse to yell at your parents.

_____ Jesus' example.

_____ The desires of your peer group.

What did you find out? Most likely, you had a mixture of expressions. Any comments about your obedience level?

OBEDIENCE OBSTACLES

Every Christian needs the character trait of obedience. If Gideon had not possessed it, he would have lost that battle.

God gives great advice. His written Word contains it. We just need to read it. Check out what God told Joshua (Joshua 1:6-9).

Back to you. Obstacles—those things that stop us from reaching a goal—prevent us from going any further. What are your obedience obstacles that keep you from being a more obedient person? Maybe some of the following obstacles are ones you struggle with.

1. ATTITUDE—Have you taken an attitude check lately? Is it good, bad, or indifferent? Disobedience thrives in an atmosphere of bad attitudes. Just like a fire when you throw gasoline on it.

Your attitude is influenced by your faith. The more you seek Christ the more your attitude will change.

Read Luke 12:31. What does it say? Seek after God. The more you seek God's kingdom through Christ, the better your attitude will be—your attitude about yourself, your parents, your friends, everything. Then obedience won't be quite as hard.

2. BAD ADVICE—Are you a sucker

for bad advice? Do you listen to your friends so much you'll believe anything they tell you?

If so, wake up! There are ghosts floating around, sliming people with bad advice. Just waiting for a new sucker.

Mostly you get it from kids with bad attitudes. People who are down on their families. People who hate their teachers. People who don't care about their faith. People who are . . . (you finish the list).

Don't be a sucker for bad advice. Read Proverbs 12:5. Notice the point? Wicked people give bad advice. And they will deceive you with it.

3. STUBBORNNESS — When was the last time you heard, "You're so stubborn"? Parents say it to us. Friends say it. Teachers say it. We all face the temptation to stiffen up our necks and make our own rules.

Stubbornness keeps us from God. Read Jesus' advice in Matthew 7:7-8. The more stubborn we become, the less we ask, seek, and knock. When we stop seeking and asking and knocking, we more easily disobey.

Don't be so stubborn about everything. Lighten up! Mellow out. Try spreading cooperation around. That's being a friend of obedience.

4. REBELLION — Here's another one of those "You're so..." words. Ever been told, "You're so rebellious"?

Read Genesis 2–3. It's a great story of rebellion. There are Adam and Eve with all the good things of life at their fingertips. Just one little thing to follow — they couldn't make the rules. They had to obey God.

Then Eve hears, *Go ahead and change the rules. Don't listen to God.*

Then the taste of rebellion was complete. God acted swiftly. Just like your parents act sometimes when you rebel.

God is the maker of the rules. Not us. When we disobey, we pay the consequence. Plain and simple.

Are you hearing the call to rebel? Marching straight forward with that stern face and forceful fist? Careful.

Rebellion is disobedience at its worst. You will face the consequences. Read Galatians 6:7-8. You reap what you sow.

TAKE THE DARE
Read Romans 12. Rewrite the chapter as if Paul were writing it to you. And remember—the consequence of disobedience is usually severe.

THE GREATEST OF THESE
CHAPTER TWELVE

Dear Abby:

I'm only 13. I need your advice. I think I'm in love. I don't understand these feelings. His name is Chip. I met him when I tried out for the play we are doing at school. I saw him . . . he saw me . . . BINGO!

We talk about everything together. Our parents won't let us go out on a date. Mostly, we meet at the mall, or at school. It's hard to hang up the phone and say good-bye to him. I've been yelled at about that.

Today he kissed me. I didn't know if I

should let him. It just happened. A thousand explosions went off. I've never, ever felt that feeling before.

Abby, is it all right to get physical with someone you love? I hear my friends talking about it. My body tells me it's the right thing to do. My heart wants to say yes, but my faith tells me God wants me to take it slow. I'm so confused. Please write me soon.

Marcia

Dear Abby:

I'm in junior high. I hope you will read this. It's about my dad. He's the most wonderful person I know. I care about him so much. I would do anything to help him be happy.

It's his job. The company he works for makes him travel a lot. I don't see him much. He's home on weekends, but then he is so tired, we don't ever do much together.

Abby, why does Dad have to work so

hard? I don't understand. I need him to be home more. Can you help me?

Cynthia

Dear Abby:

I need your advice. Bet you don't get many letters from someone in middle school. My name is Brian. I go to a school that's really big. I have some good friends there.

Abby, I've noticed that people aren't very nice sometimes. I see people hurting others at school. Laughing at them. Making jokes. Putting them down. Scaring them. Starting gossip. Ignoring people.

I've learned that God wants us to care about everyone. We are told to respect one another. I try to do that. But why are people so mean? Why don't they care about other people? I don't know what to do. I just know it isn't right. Can you help me with my problem?

Brian

Ever want to write letters like these? Ever feel so strongly for someone that you knew you were in love? So strongly for a parent? So strongly for others? All of these letters had something to do with love. Let's check it out.

KINDS OF LOVE

You might not know, but there are different kinds of love.

Marcia is experiencing one kind of love. It's romantic love—a sexual love, an attraction to someone of the opposite sex. It can really fire up your burners. It's very powerful. It's also very, very dangerous outside of God's plan.

Cynthia has a different kind of love. It is family love—a deep and caring feeling toward family members. It can be very strong when our families are close and caring.

Brian has a third kind of love. It's the most special love of all. It's Christian love, better known as *agape* love. Jesus taught us about Christian love through

His example. He told us to love one another.

Agape love is the ultimate character trait of the Christian.

LOVE'S BINDING POWER

In the last 11 chapters you have reflected on several character traits of a Christian teenager.

You looked at honesty, respect, trust, forgiveness, courage, patience, perseverance, self-control, faithfulness, reverence, and obedience. You worked on making those 11 traits part of your life.

Now we come to love. It's the trait that holds everything together. The glue that makes Christian character strong. Without love there is no character.

HOW'S YOUR LOVE LIFE?

Why does everyone always ask us about our love life? Especially when we don't have anyone. Zippo. Zero. No romance at all.

Ask yourself that question in a different way. "How's my love life when it comes to loving people in a Christian way?" Your answer to that can be very different. It doesn't depend on a romance with another person. It depends on how deep a relationship you have with God.

Draw an arrow up or an arrow down as you reflect on these attributes of a Christian love life. Up is a yes vote. Down is a no vote.

____ I treat everyone with kindness.
____ I am able to forgive people.
____ I have respect for my parents and other adults.
____ I put myself in God's hands in risky situations.
____ I am patient.
____ I have stick-to-itiveness and get the job done.
____ I have self-control and say no to temptation.
____ I am a faithful friend and loyal to my family.
____ I show reverence by acknowledging God's presence.

_____ I am obedient to those in authority over me.
_____ I can be trusted.
_____ I am honest in everything.

"Wait a minute," you say, "that looks like a list of all the stuff in this book." Right on! Love is a reflection of the other 11 character traits. The more you show each of them the greater your love. It's that simple.

TAKE THE DARE

Get out a sheet of paper. Write a letter to God, thanking Him for all the good in your life. Thank Him for making you special. Thank Him for the gift of Jesus. Thank Him that you have an opportunity to be a Christian.

Ask God to strengthen these 12 character traits. To make them rock solid. Then close your letter letting God know that you love Him. Put the letter inside your Bible. Read it often. Revise it when you need to. And always remember that God loves you and wants you to grow in Christian character.